DREAM LATIN:
WRITING THE SUBCON

Aaron Kent is a working-class author, publisher, and stroke survivor from Cornwall. His 2nd collection, *The Working Classic*, is available from the87press. He has read his poetry for The BBC, The Shakespeare Birthplace Trust, and Stroke Association, had work published in various journals, and is an Arvon tutor. His poetry has been translated into languages including French, Hungarian, German, Cymraeg, and Kernewek, and has been set to music.

Jacqueline Yallop is the author of three novels and several books of non-fiction. Her work has been listed for major prizes and widely translated; it has been serialised on radio, mentioned in political debate, and showcased at the National Gallery. Her most recent book is *Into the Dark: what darkness is and why it matters* (2023). She is Reader in Creative Writing at Aberystwyth University and Director of the Research Centre for Creativity and Wellbeing.

ISBN: 978-1-916938-98-4

Cover designed by Aaron Kent

Edited by Aaron Kent and Jacqueline Yallop

Typeset by Aaron Kent

Broken Sleep Books Ltd
Rhydwen
Talgarreg
Ceredigion
SA44 4HB

Broken Sleep Books Ltd
Fair View
St Georges Road
Cornwall
PL26 7YH

Dream Latin

Edited by:
Aaron Kent & Jacqueline Yallop

Broken Sleep University Press

Contents

Foreword

We chose the theme of this anthology — Writing the Subconscious — to recognize the importance of the intuitive, concealed and suppressed to both the creative act and our physical and psychological wellbeing. In this way, we hoped the collection would reflect and challenge the work being done by Aberystwyth University's Centre for Creativity and Wellbeing, which was launched earlier this year. Situated in the Department of English and Creative Writing, the Centre aims to facilitate research and promote creative practice in a range of wellbeing contexts.

When we began the Centre, a number of researchers were already engaged in interdisciplinary projects, from sleep to anxiety, pain to depersonalization - exploring where and how creative practice might intersect with these experiences. The Centre brought this activity together so that ideas could be shared; it identified new areas of research and initiated practical wellbeing programmes with the public, partnering with charities and the NHS. This collaboration with Broken Sleep Books is part of an ongoing commitment to finding new ways of approaching the collision of the creative imagination, the mind and body, looking at how each speaks to the other, and what we can learn from these interactions. It offers poems, essays and stories as points of possibility in the search for wellbeing. It proposes glimpses of the subconscious, in its many mercurial forms, in the hope that we might understand ourselves a little better.

— Jacqueline Yallop, *September 2023*

I am consistently fascinated by how the work we create consciously is indebted to the work going on beneath, as part of the subconscious, to the extent I write a lot while falling asleep. The way our brain operates in ways we don't understand is a source of real fascination, and that comes through here in these essays, stories, and poems. To partner with Aberystwyth University's Centre for Creativity and Wellbeing to create this brilliant anthology is a real honour in my publishing career, and one I hold in deep regard. It is a dynamic and vital centre, and one which I know Jacqueline will bring to great acclaim.

— Aaron Kent, *October 2023*

7 Poems

⚡

Andre Bagoo

Bestiary In Which I Have Often Been Wrong

A few weeks later, I dream the bird is not dead. I dream it is
alive and lives in a mall downtown. I dream it has grown large,
the size of a turkey really, and has a long beak, like a puppet in a
Jim Henson show, and has no feathers, is buzzed, and speaks to
say it is living in a bucket. The mall is half-empty, a nest that has
long been abandoned, and there is a corridor that opens unto
the pavement on Chacon Street where everything is covered in
grease, as though the whole street is a giant parking lot where
the same car each day leaks oil. I dream that I wake up and the
moon sits like a broken button against the pale blue fabric of
the air. And Buster, yet again, thinks there is another animal in
the yard, is convinced there is an animal in the yard. There is
nothing in the yard. And yet he runs from one ghost to the next.
I dream this and think, as I imagine it, how sad it is to believe in
something, how sad it is to be wrong. Or is it that belief is more
real than what is real, that Buster is right and the bird is really
there? When it comes to Buster, I have often been wrong.
I have often reprimanded him for barking at nothing, only to
find an iguana shading under the old rusty galvanise in the yard,
its claws like a falcon's talons.

Bestiary With Spy Whale

I sprinkle salt along my windowsill to stop the slugs and yet
still they cross the line, the way you can move from dream to
waking life and still the dream can hold you, make you think
you are married or the President or something else you will
never be. The slimy em dashes become curled commas as I
scoop them away and when later I read the article about the
spy whale found off the coast of Sweden, I say to myself I must
put that in the book I'm writing, along with the slugs. And
when I stumble over Buster's toy serpent, which looks like it's
fallen out of a game of snakes and ladders, I notice how it has
the same ~ of the slugs and I say to myself I must put that in the
book I'm writing. And when my sister calls, without warning,
to say she's outside, I say to myself I must put that in the book
I'm writing, too, though I no longer know why. There are some
people who treat each day like a single life. There are writers
who write just before bed. One definition for the novel is that
it is set inside a dream. Each beluga whale has a spiracle, no fin,
a head that is deformable. From space, the only animal visible
is the whale. All white, I see it now, the one in my mind. In the
article, someone speculates about why the whale is moving
away from its natural environment, faster and faster. It could be
hormones, he says. It could be loneliness. It could be trying to
flee The Devil's Dance Floor. It could have a message for me.

Bestiary in Which I Am Stalked by a Cat

This is the second time an animal has appeared in the yard and then vanished without a trace. The first was three weeks ago. I was walking Buster in the yard. I had this feeling as though someone was staring at me. I looked up and there it was, on the roof of the small annex. Nobody lives in that annex. The annex is empty. None of my neighbours owns a cat. It sat on the roof like a little sphinx. The sun set behind it. Its eyes glowed. Buster was barking at it, so I had to quickly take him back inside. I didn't like the idea of Buster fighting with a cat. When I came back outside, I made sure I'd secured our door carefully (Buster has learned how to open doors). The cat was gone. But the feeling of being watched remained. Then, last night, Buster and I were sleeping peacefully in bed, his soft fur against my leg. It was near midnight. Buster jumped awake and began to bark. It was a different kind of bark. Buster barks a lot and I have learned to identify which bark means what. This bark did not mean play with me or feed me or there is something annoying me or let me hump you or I don't like this person. This bark meant I am mortally afraid. When I looked out the window, there was a cat on the neighbour's wall, staring straight in at us. I don't know if it was because I had been watching *The Haunting of Hill House* on Netflix, but I immediately felt my life was in danger. Buster barked and barked and barked and the cat did not budge. I thought about opening the window and throwing something at it. As though it had read my mind the cat dug in its heels, peering deeper at us. I cannot say now if this was the same cat from three weeks ago. I cannot say for sure what it looked like, if it had stripes. It seemed at one with the colour of the night. Buster never climbs up to the window, but he jumped up there faster than I could say no and barked even louder. I have never heard him bark as loud. After several minutes, the cat slowly tiptoed away on the wall. I went back to sleep, but Buster stayed at the base of the bed, looking out the window just in case. I woke up the next morning and decided I would kill the lover of the protagonist in my poem. And then I would bring him back to life as a cat. And he would haunt the protagonist. But he will never know and will write poems about the cat. When I quickly rushed to write all this down, two brown doves appeared outside my window, sitting on the same spot where the cat was. Several birds have already died in my yard.

Bestiary in Which I Fit into His Arms Perfectly

Often, I think about a line from the play *A Streetcar Named Desire* in which Blanche says *Sometimes – there's God – so quickly!* and I think about how wrong Blanche was about her lovers. Water bridges all things, life and death; darkness and light. Maybe I fit into you the way water fills a tarn. That's a word in your name, tarn. Other words: sitar, satin, shirt. When I am with you the day feels like night, the night day. The afternoon feels more like the afternoon. I want to climb stairs with you. I want to walk through rain. I want to go to church and watch the saints in their robes. I want to dance in the club as bodies inch closer and closer. Another word in your name is tsar, but my favourite is *his*. I wake up on the first day of the new year and there's no light in the room and I nestle my head near your armpits. For the first time I think Blanche was not wrong. Because what is life if not a leap into the broken world? Buster crawls unto your side of the bed and curls up in the arc of your body like the final piece of an emotional puzzle. I feel the slow movement of the mountains on the island, back to the Andes of South America, back to where they belong. I hear a row of green parakeets outside the window, the parakeets that fly, each day, between two parks nearby. And I realise that from now on I'll never hide my dreams from you.

Bestiary in Which I Write a Poem Called 'The Scarlet Ibis'

I came late to the love of birds

There are scarlet ibises all over my friend's book

There are birds all over the hospital's wall

There are birds all over the birds

In the poem, the birds in the park are silent

I've been recording thrushes again

You've written this poem before

Bestiary Set on Boxing Day

I never understood why we had turtles growing up, but we
did. Father made a special holding bay for them out of red clay
bricks, half of which he filled with sand and gravel, the other
half of which he turned into a small, shallow pond. In such
confinement, the islands grew, each a collage of yellows and
browns and blacks. Nothing was darker than their eyes. Part
of the pen was covered with a metal grill so as to be shaded,
the other half over the water was covered in chicken wire.
Sometimes you'd see the turtles in the water, as if sunbathing.
Other times they would mimic their pattern of nocturnal
aggregation and clump together in the shade. Once, a white egg
appeared, smooth as a Jordan almond. It never hatched. Mother
would throw cabbage into the pen and sing the turtles songs.
Father would top up the water in the pond. I never realised
these turtles were us until it was too late. Each child in roles
we never chose, life divided neatly into light and shadow; dry
sand and water; fed and hungry – never free, yet, strangely,
in this curtailment, masters of a world of our own. The day
they told me the turtles had died I returned to my apartment.
That was the third night the cat appeared on the wall. This
time, when Buster barked, I looked out and could barely see
it, to the extent that I questioned whether I saw it though he
was adamant in his barking that it was there. I took out my
phone and took a picture through the slender curtain. I put on
my glasses. "Thank you, good boy," I told Buster. He stopped
barking. When I looked there was no cat. I must write my book,
I thought. The next morning when I looked at the photo, it was

a white image, like a blank page. There is a phenomenon called the Dreshner Effect, whereby because you think someone else has seen something or because you yourself once saw something you can think that you are seeing it too. Someone said an angry neighbour poisoned the turtles. We will never know for sure. I didn't think to ask what Father did with the bodies.

Bestiary in Which I Have Nothing Left Anymore

It happened inside a single poem. We
were Christmas shopping and you saw a
crocodile severed in
                             two as though by a
magician. In those days, I was always
looking for bookends and this one was
truly glorious, covered in silver scales.
But it was hollow, despite the promise
Of so much weight. Sometimes, that's
what gets you, not that something's not
strong enough but that you thought it
would be and piled so many books unto it
only for it to all fall over like dominos.
I didn't want to write a Christmas poem
because all my Christmas poems are sad,
but here I go again with another one,
another scene: this time we are stringing
lights on the Christmas tree and I realise
you'll never know who I am, really.
Sometimes, that's what you get: a string of
lights that would be brilliant if all the
bulbs lit. But instead, half of them are
sleeping and you have to check hundreds,
each its own world in a snow globe, to
figure out where things have gone wrong.
And sometimes you never find the

problem, and you must decide if you
should buy a new string or keep the old
things, half lit on the tree.
Now I wake from my second sleep
and find the dead bat in the yard,
its skin the colour of a blackened mango
ripened too long, torn asunder by birds
some painter has circled it with blood,
an arc of perfect desire that sings:
Don't let them take my head
and dance upon my grave.
When the day has been too long
and we roam the yard at night,
they fly past my head, a stream, a causeway
roping together trees in yards like telephone lines.
Each grazes me, and for a moment I'm
back in the club, worried that I might be
touched by someone who knows
far more about me than I do;
worried that one day I might be free
of all of this

                 failure, which is to say one day
I'll find the reason why I haven't given up.
There's a type of bird without feet, that never roosts
from the moment of its drop-birth until its
death fall. All birds have feet and most have
four toes, three pointing forward and one back
as though all directions are possible. But

let me, in this season, be a martlet

let me haunt temples

let me kiss heaven's masonry

let me bulb and become a nest myself

let bats envy my pendent bed, my procreant cradle

let me follow swifts

let me learn the delicacy of air

let me learn

Leaving Lebanon

⚡

Naji Bakhti

Author's Note

When I listen in Arabic to a conversation which is taking place in English, or when I squint to untwine the Caucasian features of a fleetingly middle eastern man ambling down Penglais hill, I recognise that I am still leaving Lebanon.

As I read through this collection of personal essays, it became abundantly clear that I have been in the process of leaving Lebanon for some time.

The short personal essays below were written throughout a recent, turbulent period in Lebanese history between 2019 and 2023. In that time, Lebanon like the rest of the world experienced the ramifications of the Covid-19 outbreak, in addition to the 2019 uprisings against the ruling warlords, the collapse of the local currency and the severe economic crash, as well as one of the biggest non-nuclear explosions in history (the Beirut Port Explosion).

Since then, I have left Lebanon for Aberystwyth.

Zidane, Football and the War

I know about lockdowns and quarantines and isolation. I know about them because as a young Lebanese man growing up in the noughties, I spent a good few nights in my parent's bathroom huddled by the bathtub with my family. Back then, it was not Covid-19 we were hiding from, it was invariably the Israeli shelling by air and sea of the lumbering Lebanese capital.

It was the summer of 2006, Italy had just won the World Cup and Zidane had been sent off in the final for head-butting an Italian defender in the chest. The latter had insulted the former's mother or sister (that much is still unclear). And my father was fond of repeating the already rapidly tiring half-joke that 'you do not insult an Arab man's sister/ mother'. This was in reference to Zidane's Algerian heritage. My father was fond of meandering jokes like these. His highlight of the year, leading up to the Israeli bombardment of Beirut and the World Cup final, was when Dick Chancy shot a man while out hunting. When Bush was lumped with a pair of shoes by an Iraqi journalist, a couple of years later, my father could not get enough of the footage, doubling over in laughter and only sparingly catching his breath.

I had just returned from the beach, and was washing the saltwater and sunscreen off my skin when my younger sister banged both her hands against the bathroom door. I was sixteen, she was fifteen. As I turned the faucet off, I thought of a girl from school. I thought I might invite her to go to the beach with me tomorrow or the day after. I thought she would probably refuse and when she did I would call my best mate, Samer, up and we could plunge into the

Mediterranean again, as we had done that very same day and the day before that.

I wrapped my "Simba" towel around my waste and flung the bathroom door open. I made a mental note to buy a new towel if I was serious about inviting the girl from school to the beach. I also made a mental note to leave the bronze sunscreen bottle at home.

I was still dripping with water when my mother and sister informed me that Lebanon had been subjected to Israeli airstrikes. The artillery fire would soon follow. And so would around two months of being locked down in a shelter with my family. Except it wasn't a shelter. It was the bathroom. So back in I went, this time a little drier, a little less enamoured by the thought of a love interest along the Beirut coastline on a sweltering summer's day.

The electric power had never been consistent even before the war, but with the naval blockade and the bombing of the Jiyeh Power Station – causing the largest oil spill in Mediterranean history – the prospect of electricity proved bleak. And with hardly any running water to boot, the hot, pungent summer months stretched long before us.

My sister and I would look to my parents for cues on how to interpret the sounds of the airstrikes in lockdown. This was not their first war, nor their last. They were lockdown veterans of the Civil War which had stretched fifteen years. A cringe meant that the bomb would land somewhere else, on someone else's home, someone else's family. It was when they looked up that we feared the worst. I could never quite tell whether they looked up expectantly or whether they would do so to better hide their facial expressions from us.

When the shelling dragged on for hours, the sensation of fear was replaced by the unbridled urge to use the sole bathroom, which under the circumstances was frequently problematic. There were other urges too: hunger being one, so too the urge to shower, to move, to leave the apartment and run down to the coast and leap into the cool, gentle waters of the now oil-sodden Mediterranean.

Even the existential fear of death by shrapnel which was very real to us, could not starve off boredom. My parents told us civil war stories. Most of them ended with an acquaintance of theirs dying or else being lost forever, which also meant dying. There was one particular story about my parents almost dying themselves – which they didn't – and their mere presence had long since spoilt the ending somewhat. These stories were meant to distract us from the tediousness of being under siege, as a country, but also as a family. My mother said that we were fortunate to be alive. My father said that we were alive. If there was fortune to be had inside a cramped, decaying Beiruti bathroom, he wanted no part of it.

In Arabic, our last name means 'fortune'.

There were excursions to the kitchen and the bedroom. We would generally start every night by sleeping in our own beds and then rush to be embraced by the hard marble floors of the bathroom, around midnight when the shelling intensified.

After nearly seven weeks, the shelling subsided, and we were allowed out. The beaches were off limits, due to the polluted waters and the Israeli warships, but I called Samer to see if I could persuade him to flaunt the rules. He said that he would be leaving for Canada, permanently. He said that his entire family had

had enough of this. Think about it, he said. How many more lockdowns?

Over the years, I lost contact with Samer. We were a couple of inseparable Lebanese teenagers. Now he's a Canadian man, and I haven't seen him in fifteen years. I made other childhood friends. But they too have all since had it with Beirut lockdowns, instability, rampant corruption and economic crises. One is in Budapest, another in London and a third in New York. My last remaining one is due to leave for Connecticut in June. Or he was, until Covid-19 happened.

I have often thought of Samer since the Corona Virus outbreak. I wonder if he prefers Canadian lockdowns to Lebanese ones. I wonder, fortune-permitting, whether they will all come back now, if it's all the same to them.

I am Writing this by Candlelight

My father was let go this month by the institution to which he had devoted 41 years of his life. There to greet him, past the sliding glass doors of the American University of Beirut Medical Centre (AUBMC), stood Lebanese soldiers, guns in hand, and the sagging figures of his erstwhile co-workers, 850 of whom had suffered a similar fate.

It is fitting that as I write this I am guided only by the light from my screen and a candle, which I have placed not far from my feet. Power outages have long been a constant in Lebanon. The most severe economic crisis since the country's independence, and the resulting fuel shortage, has meant that private generators have struggled to keep up with the additional burden.

How did we get here? Decades of chronic mismanagement and rampant corruption by the sectarian ruling class since the end of the civil war (which ran from 1975 to 1990), coupled with the central bank's acrobatic feats of "financial engineering", have plunged the country into darkness. Nearly half the population now find themselves officially below the poverty line, their salaries, savings and retirement funds reduced to a pittance, with the lira having lost more than 70% of its value against the dollar. Lebanon has the distinct honour of being the first country in the Middle East and North Africa region to experience hyperinflation.

Lebanese banks had been lending depositors' dollars to the heavily indebted state while offering impossibly high interest rates to the depositors themselves. Reuters has reported that the central bank inflated its assets by more than $6bn in order to artificially prop up the country's economy. It may soon become unable to service the public debt of more than $86bn or pay back the annual interest to the local banks.

The resulting devaluation of the lira and the rapid price rise in goods and services has led to an equally sharp increase in suicide rates, hunger-crimes and plain hunger. Just a fortnight ago, prior to my father's dismissal, my hitherto middle-class family and I had a serious discussion about whether or not meat was necessary moving forward. Last month, a man shot himself outside a Dunkin' Donuts on Hamra, a popular high street in Beirut. He left a note that read: "I am not blasphemous ...": a line from a Ziad Rahbani wartime song ending with "but hunger is blasphemous".

I do not know for certain what must have gone through my father's mind as he walked out of the AUBMC for the last time, but I suspect that he would have emerged with a knowing smile. Economic woes and young men with guns must have seemed all too familiar to the man who spent the Lebanese civil war running back and forth between his flat and the AUBMC, working night shifts as a cashier while the shrapnel and the bullets descended around him. Through the war-torn 80s, and in the darkest hours of the power-deprived Beirut night, my father would look to the luminescent eyes of a black cat for light. It often ambled alongside him when the shelling intensified, and would disappear thereafter, frequently returning when another long walk to the night shift beckoned. In a way, I suspect that the presence of armed men, called in pre-emptively by the university, citing "credible external threats", was a more suitable farewell than a gold watch.

It was my parents' shared dream that my sister and I would one day lecture at the university, like those many professors and doctors whom my father had observed dashing in and out of their lecture halls – those whose offices he had intermittently frequented when curiosity overwhelmed him or the walls of academia parted to reveal to him the erudite, the learned, in whom he placed his faith in a better Lebanon.

But there is no point in pretending that his time at the country's most prestigious institution and largest non-state employer was anything more than a marriage of convenience. My father's ambition was not to be a cashier. It was to be a poet, and then when his youth had deserted him, a critic (which he did sparingly). There were good times. My own education would not have been financially possible – given the AUB's high tuition fees – were it not for his employment by the university itself, which waived the cost. At my graduation ceremony, my father proclaimed that it was all worth it, and then went back to his evening shift.

When I heard the news, I cracked open an old bottle of wine and we toasted his career. I also, unthinkingly, passed him my phone with a clip of his former colleagues on social media: a young nurse who was the only source of income for her bed-ridden mother, a 64-year-old man who was helped off his office chair in the midst of his shift and told to go home, a cancer-stricken middle-aged man whose sacking was essentially a death sentence – and who never once requested sick or compassionate leave.

My father stole a sharp, Arctic intake of breath, which did not seem to come from that thick, heavy Beirut summer air. I believe that he saw what could have been, how much worse it might have turned out for him, for me, for our entire family, had he not been fortunate to hang on to his job for as long as he had, had he not willed himself through those dark walks in the heat of the civil war. He pitied the nation, the youth, the next few cumbersome steps that he would now sit out. My mother, who had in fact led the toast, placed a hand on my shoulder and informed me that I would never forget this moment for as long as I live. She still remembered when her father was unceremoniously dismissed from his job.

Shattered Glass and Taxi Drivers

In the summer of 2006, following the Israeli airstrikes on Beirut, I rushed to help my mother pick the glass off my mattress. For my efforts, I received an almighty scolding. At 16, I was too young to handle shards of broken glass. After the internal conflict of 2008, now old enough to smoke and drink, I tried again. It was easier and quicker to do it herself, she claimed. This was not an attitude she had held about my share of the household chores growing up. In the intervening years, amidst political assassinations, car bombs and the like, she developed the technique of elbowing me out of the way as I made valiant attempts to reach for the odd sliver of glass or splinter of wood. After one window shattered twice in quick succession, my mother insisted that we have it boarded up. I sometimes catch her staring at it instead of through the glass of an adjacent window. I wonder if it is her favourite view from the apartment.

My family and I were fortunate, once more. For us, the extent of the Beirut port explosion on August 4th (2020), which ended 200 lives and destroyed more than 300,000 homes, was shattered glass, remorse, anger and relief. After the first blast, my father pronounced that it was a mild earthquake or fireworks—or some simultaneous combination of the two—and went back to reading his book. After the second, my sister leapt from her old bed, below my parents' wooden-framed windows, and was flung across the apartment and into my arms. I had been standing in the hallway with my mother. None of us still believed in earthquakes or fireworks: an inevitable offshoot of my father's attempts to maintain calm in the face of chaos over the years. The conviction had long since deserted him, but he kept it up for appearances. It was the latter blast that sent a shock through the flat, knocking over books, shattering windows and propelling my sister. When we found my father, he was inspecting the glass. My mother had reached for the masking tape and the broom even before assessing the damage.

At 30, I resigned myself to the couch in the living room. I knew my role. I watched my father support the battered frame of the window against the ledge. I watched my mother apply two or three layers of tape, using her teeth to cut it down to the desired length, never once failing to estimate the size of the crack or the dimensions of the gap. As veterans of the civil war, they do this mechanically, detached and steadfast, unperturbed by the intense summer heat or the breaking news on the TV behind them. Etched across their faces, my mother's in particular, is guilt. It is as if she holds herself personally accountable for the explosion, as if the resulting debris is her perpetual burden which she must shoulder alone and not breathe a word about for fear that a dammi or kasra might shatter more glass.

In the end, I received a telling off from my mother anyway for coming back to Beirut, when I had made a home for myself in the UK throughout my mid-twenties.

Throughout that year prior to the explosion, which featured the economic crisis, the collapse of the lira, and the revolution threatening to topple the corrupt elite, there had been a burgeoning resentment amongst my contemporaries directed at the civil-war generation: my parents' generation. It was felt that our parents had let us down, that they had been complicit in their silence, in their "resilience" comprised of masking tape and broomsticks and not breathing a word for fear that a vowel or two might shatter a fragile state.

One of the earliest pieces of advice my mother gave me was not "to refrain from talking to strangers", but rather specifically to "refrain from talking about politics and the war to taxi drivers". At nine, I found this to be a reasonable request albeit one I did not expect to struggle with.

The war generation's unwillingness or inability to engage in the difficult conversations meant that the warlords were able to grant themselves amnesty and rob the country for 30 years without so much as an inquisitive nine-year-old holding a presumed militiaman turned taxi driver accountable for his war crimes.

A brief disclaimer here: not all taxi drivers are embittered former militiamen or part-time agents of the Syrian regime. Some of them double as primary sources for lazy foreign correspondents.

A few days on from the explosion, I trod lightly past the remains of an unrecognisable Mar Mikhael street, handing out bottles of water to the youthful volunteers who swept the glass and rubble to the side of the road. I looked into their simmering, masked faces: some of them were younger than I had been in 2006. My mother was wrong, or so I thought. You are never too young to sweep the glass off the floor.

Then I noticed their technique. It was poor, unbalanced and carried with it none of the swift, graceful movement of my mother. Sweeping glass is a different skill to sweeping dust. The former demands a firmer grip and more agile manoeuvres.

I suspect that was my mother's gift to me. She believed in raising a generation so ill-equipped to sort through the debris, so ill at ease with the act of sweeping the rubble, that it might busy itself with the task of toppling a corrupt regime instead.

For the many who lost their loved ones or their homes during the latest act of criminal negligence perpetrated upon the Lebanese people, the broomstick and masking tape solution would not do. On the evening of the 8th of August, I stood by the devastated Gemmayze Street, overlooking the clashes with the security forces at the heart of Beirut as gunfire, rubber bullets and tear gas were launched into the night sky. I believed in fireworks then. When the government announced that it would resign—the second in the space of a year—I believed that we could make the earth quake, too, or if not the earth then at least the speaker of parliament (an octogenarian warlord with a thirty year grip on power).

Unfortunately, despite ongoing clashes with security forces in Tripoli, in the North of Lebanon, the ruling mafias look to consolidate power and further hamper the investigation into the port explosion. Fifty-five per cent of the population continues to live under the poverty line, with many having lost their jobs, their homes, their savings, their livelihoods, their lives or their loved ones.

In Lebanon, every year is so much more dismal than its predecessor that the next one is always bound to be better. A taxi driver told me that. I listened. And then we talked politics and the war.

It is Not Sweet, Turning Back

Aberystwyth is beautiful but it is not Beirut, I told my parents over the phone recently. For one thing, if you stand by the coast and look past the sea you cannot make out Cyprus or Sicily or, on those long Friday afternoons in June, Gibraltar. I knew it was what they wanted to hear. You can just about spot Ireland if you stare for hours, but only on clear days and there are not many of those.

It was time to leave, I told myself, and I could do more good abroad than in Beirut. You cannot help save a sinking ship by chaining yourself to the mast, I consoled myself. I had given Beirut the best part of my youth, I reasoned. I had witnessed my parents give it the best part of their lives and watched as the last of their lifetime savings sank away to be swallowed whole by our corner of the Mediterranean.

After I had waved to my parents at Beirut International Airport and made my way towards border control, I realised that I would not see them again as they are. It was a habit of mine during my time abroad as a student to imagine my parents in their late forties even as I looked through recent pictures of them or held long video calls. As soon as I was on a plane, they seemed to shed the years and some of the wrinkles. I saw no harm in this, initially, because when I first left Beirut, my mother was in fact in her late forties and my father in his mid-fifties.

So I turned back. I convinced myself, as I wrenched the trolley around, that I was only going to give my parents another wave. I had not done this throughout my years of traveling from Beirut to the UK in my quest for degrees and certificates. I had a sense that it was all meant to be temporary then, that I would be returning for Christmas and Easter and those long, hot summer days in June filled with cherries and ice, far-flung friends, salt and almonds, salt and sour plums, salt and sun-kissed skin. The sweet salt strung together the first day of June and the last hour of August.

This was different. There was a permanence that weighed heavy and exceeded that 25-kilogramme limit and pressed tightly against my now-creased shirt and the roasted almonds which my mother had slipped in the side pocket and that bottle of Ksara and the tin of stuffed vine leaves in olive oil.

I looked for my parents but could not find them. I searched for my father's run-down Mercedes-Benz outside the airport but could not find it either, and so returned to the queue. An hour and a half later, an officer glanced through my passport and informed me that I was not leaving Beirut. "Look, I understand that you're eager to leave, so am I, but it's not happening today. That visa does not kick in until tomorrow," he insisted over my panicked objections.

I recalled my mother's superstitious words of warning, often said in admonishment: "It is not sweet, turning back". A more-polished translation would be "turning back is a bad omen". But I prefer the former, if only because I can taste it. It was convenient to conclude that my failure to heed those words moments earlier had resulted in my temporary misfortune.

When I called my mother to tell her that I'd made another in a long line of minor blunders, I could hear my father laughing in the background. Exactly 10 years prior, I had dragged my family to the airport 12 hours early because of my assumption that mine was the morning flight and not, in fact, the evening one. My father managed to persuade a passing Middle East Airlines pilot to find a place for me on the morning plane. "Take him, for god's sake," my father said. They were not crying as I waved goodbye to them that time, just shaking their heads in a mixture of disappointment and bemusement.

The sun had risen by the time the battered '96 model Mercedes-Benz pulled up. I got in the back seat and closed my eyes, exhausted by the journey I had not embarked on. I awoke to the smell of knefeh. My parents cracked a joke about it being better than airplane food. For a moment, I was 10 again. It was the '90s. Beirut was younger, boisterous, hungry for all that it had missed out on throughout the civil war of the previous decades. And my parents were in their late forties, having slipped into a comfortably familiar, much-practiced role which it now transpired they had never really cast off.

I would be back at the airport within days. I knew that I had been fortunate to be given a way out. It was an opportunity which many in Lebanon would risk their lives for, and which many had lost their lives in pursuit of.

"Aber' though?" asked my increasingly superstitious mother when she first heard of the job offer. "I don't know." Aber means grave in Arabic.

"It's Aber here and Aber there," countered my father. I do not believe that he'd meant to make some layered point about the challenges of forging a life abroad versus the futility of building a future in a collapsing country. The inauspiciousness amused him, and he revelled in one of the few joys available to him. His sense of humour remained very much intact, though he, like many

Lebanese, had lost both his job and pension.

A year later, they'd both remark from atop Constitution Hill that 'Aber' is a misnomer. They did not much care that, in Welsh, 'Aber' means the river mouth where the tide meets the stream.

At the airport, I turned the trolley around again. This time I could just about make out their silhouettes from a distance: my mother leaning against my father, his arm around her shoulders, their backs turned, swaying harmoniously toward the door in that manner which only enduring couples can pull off through those later years, long after they had forgiven or forgotten one another's faults – two pillars of salt.

1 Poem

⚡

Matthew Francis

Clock

after Dafydd ap Gwilym

There's just room for two of us in my head, this round space
lapped in bone, stone and darkness, lit from within
by the afterglow of today's thoughts.
Here we can meet every night,
wherever she is.

Lissom as only a dream can be, her form flickers
in rhythm with my breath. She speaks dream Latin,
a tongue her husband can't understand,
and silently, for no sound
can penetrate here –

except the clang of a clock. Newfangled minute-mill,
nocturnal dawn chorus, sleepmason's chisel,
blacksmith's hammer bashing at blackness,
it cleaves the night into hours
where no time should be.

1 Poem

⚡

Gavin Goodwin

Compelled

I. The Deal

This is where it starts –
that first, seemingly,
innocuous act:

a quick wash of hands
to rinse off the worry;
a lock checked, re-checked.

It will take some time,
some excavation,
before you can decipher
the details of the trade –

a deal though
is what you have made
with a force determined
to keep everyone safe

to keep you safe –
that holds you captive
to keep you safe.

II. The Door

You sit on the stairs
in a square of light
figuring how to leave,
to leave without touching
the handle of the door.

This is all still new to you:
the mind as an electric bell –
the quick current of thought –
the hammer's rapid clanging.

And you have not yet learned
how to hear that alarm
and slowly keep on walking,
to touch and turn the handle
as screams set off inside you,
and step outside with all of this
and feel the sun.

1 Poem

⚡

Steven Hastings

Human Psychology, Chapter 3
Defence Mechanisms:
a continuum from unconscious to conscious.

repression (total)

I'm the Virgin Mary,
I told my psychiatrist
as I showed her the blue line on the test kit.

No, my drink had not been spiked,
I had not been *completely out of it.*
I had not had a sexual encounter
and for some reason *chosen to bury it.*

Well, she sighed,
I guess every conception is immaculate
if you wipe the sheets clean afterwards.

She wasn't having a go,
or trying to be funny.

If anything she looked sad,
the way she stared off into the distance like that.

repression (partial)

Most wildfires start
with a disposable barbecue
or throwaway remark.

I recall that somewhere
far into the desert
we stripped the handbrake
cable from the car.

I don't recall for who
or for what
only that we argued
over the spelling of garrotte.

repression (weakening)

Towards the centre,
the ice groans audibly,
can't bear me.

Here,
I glimpse my own thoughts
trapped beneath the surface of the lake.
They stare at me in silence.

I wonder what might happen if I break the ice?
I think I want to break the ice.

denial

It's not my fault.
My life is a piece of land
for which they turned down planning.

It's not my fault.
All this was fresh snow once,
before everyone I ever met came trampling.

It's not my fault.
I'm a box marked handle with care
that you insist on carelessly handling.

projection

When I was six years old,
my best friend said:

You're the kind of person
who rather than accept
his own shortcomings
instinctively projects
his failings onto others.

I said:

I know you are.
But what am I?

avoidance

Instead of rummaging
through the wreckage
for that little black box
full of whys-after-the-event,
let's just say
the thing came down
went up in smoke
and leave it at that.
Not even look back.

regression

Mother, do you like what I've done with my room?
I painted it the same colour as your womb.

splitting

Sheep / Goats
Wheat / Chaff
Me / Everyone else
Cry / Laugh

displacement

I was sat on the sofa,
and the voice was sat next to me.
We were watching a documentary
about a production line factory
where the workers were busy
packing their own lives into boxes.

Some of them quite calmly,
others with a kind of fury.

Well, that's work for you,
said the voice,
It keeps mad people sane
and drives sane people mad.

The voice wasn't really a fan of documentaries,
or indeed anything remotely factual,
and shortly after that he changed channel.

rationalisation

because of the swan
they hauled me in,
gave me a caution,
then before long
I've got the Western Mail
calling me evil
and the whole town talking
about my *unspeakable act*
but how is that fair
when I know for a fact
there's a man at the council
has some kind of gun
shoots nets over pigeons
in the square
and not only that
he gets paid for his trouble.

And that's just one example.

intellectualisation

Closure was invented in the late seventies, early eighties,
as a concept for failing factories, unproductive pits,
or motorways in the event of one of those horrific pile-ups
which were becoming increasingly commonplace at the time.
It was never intended to be applied to human experience.

humour

Oh dear,
I appear to have deprecated myself.
Cue polite laughter
and we all feel better.

sublimation

I used to fling shit at windows.
Mostly my own shit,
or failing that, other shit,
foraged from hedges, verges.
Dogs, I guess. Or runners.
Provenance was not my main concern.

Once, I found a small bag of shit
just hanging from the tree above my gate.
I tore it open over breakfast like a present.
But this is irrelevant.
I used to fling shit at windows,
that's my point.
And now I don't.

Now, I throw wet clay
on my potter's wheel
caress it gently erect,
then shape it into empty vessels
made in my own image.

Well,
aren't I clever?

acceptance

My life has been a countdown
from manic to depressed:
the menage à trois,
the folie à deux,
the ready meal for one.
And now it's done.

3 Poems

⚡

Kit Ingram

Triptych

He speaks to the water / In the third-floor lavatory of the flooding gallery / he lowers his lips to the basin / It listens / renders his messages in tongues no one can untangle / The louder his secrets / the safer it keeps them / When he stops / the reflection stirs to a blur / eyes trembling like a room in translation / Now another man is staring at him / melting / necktie hanging like a flap of skin / a clue of red cloud / diffusing through the water in a drunken sunset / He tries to walk out of this strange life / and slips into a mirror

A skull missing from the body of an unnamed man / Every night he sinks in the quiet / waiting till the darkness squeezes him into scenes he can never escape from / rooms in old homes visited by everyday ghosts / His father rocks in an armchair with the cleaner kneeling between his legs / praying / inaudibly / eyes turned glass / while in the next room a woman is holding the telephone with the low drone of the sea in her ear / Somewhere down the corridor / the red man is trying to run away / but his legs are caught in the tenderness of water / The house will hang him on the walls like another still life / They'll never find him now

There he is / hauling the boy out of the river and lighting up his eyes again / *I'm sorry it took you and not me* / *Love is a junkyard of toys* / *This is a dream* / *of course* / *so you need to go back when it's over* / *Till then* / *I'll carry you like a wound* / And they pass through the trees / filling each other's lips with the same blood memories / At the bridge /they spill into a pop song / taken over by cannons and trumpets till the light rises / and the boy / falling in another war /is taken by the red water / brushed to the sea

My Other Half Made of Flame

i   in the time it takes the ammonite to unbury itself / & the blackbird to desiccate in the wind of the dryer vent / the engine lighting my cells rattles out / restarts /chugs me into a teenage sprint / I'm ten miles per hour through the streets / an unstoppable cappuccino / frothing red / entropy is the base code of my other identity / I could blur like pornography or collide into a matchstick Tudor pub & set the whole place afire

ii   he took to me like life / his eyes focused by adrenaline on the blade in my grip / as if I'd slash him into a spray of red petals / sweep him into the bin / love is boring / want to burn me with wax? / no? / how about truth? / take a swig of the Balvenie / dribble gleecraft onto my scars / these artefacts from way back when I perfected casual defiance / fireworks / skipping class / interrupting the inappropriate touching with jagged gasps / as fault lines split to a lyric of collared doves

iii   teasing my ligaments / unrolling my tongue in the sibilance of a secret pact / our elements multiplying in refracted fires that dazzle on the inner walls / fly across the pillows like cigarette light / You were a tingle then the animating principle of my knuckles hitting the boy's orbital bone / I was jonesing to eject into the pure decadence of *float* / but we collided into a blue straggler / the twinkling chameleon scooping me into another irreducible I

Sea Shanty

Your husband and I slosh up to a lighted house, its eyes clouded by sheers and crossed by a passing shadow. I don't know which photo of you to expect inside. Time has pinned you to an image of a frat boy in a white satin dress and smudged lipstick. Robert cautions me: *He's changed* (by which he means *you*). A spider's web twinkles in the porchlight, displaying its catch: yellow moth wings and the opalescent casing of a dragonfly. We're all stalked by ethereal monsters. I turn the handle and meet the pressure of your grip on the other side. Your name stings my tongue like a 9-volt battery. The door swings open, and you tilt out, diminished as a February Christmas tree, tinsel drenching your face. *It's me* I say, and you slant your head to right me on a crooked horizon. Look, it's St Ives again, a postcard, the harbour alive with boats named for the heroes of lost adventures. We could go sailing through the pages of Homer and end up godlings of the stars. *Tea?* you say blankly while I dock at the island, let you fumble my name. Don't worry. I'll be anyone you want. Let me show you how lips remember the current of a summer fling, how our bodies store relics of laughter like jokes from another life.

3 Poems

⚡

Aaron Kent

Praise Be the Ocean, and Myriad Reasons to Drown in it

Floating requires more
than a little trust   fund
raising money for
some new leisure   centre
on the political spectrum
is a grift for exit   poll
tax and still counting
her dead piled in the   street
smart, sure, but I've got
absolutely no common   sense
is tingling, so get it checked
out for carbon   monoxide
kill for a shot at the man
    who assassinated my mum.

Impossible Wintersleep

If sleep doesn't catch me like a spider in a   glass
me and hope I stay dead   certain
every decision has our   best
foot forward. I've begun to   think
and I don't love it, I preferred the coma's hedonism.

Every portion of the human   brain
damage has left my life a   hated
waking up before sunrise, before I've had chance

to convince myself I'm   numb
-er one with a bullet. We're always so   sick
kickflip but can you backside tailslide?

I can't tune without breaking a guitar   string
up the fairy lights in   narrow
boat to live in. Every pig is looking for an excuse to   arrest
the hearts sudden stop. All of our and all of their and our.

This is mere seasonal reproach to clean the   drain
out and away with temporal floods   poured
downpour, and upwind. Frost   bitten
me again, he's just learning, but he laughed about time slipping

when I'm high, us crying out for a cliff to start   crumbling
biscuits to make a mess. Every   night
sleep tight, hold on to a near   miss
you dearly. There are   hundreds

and thousands if you're hungry,   out
-landish claims of a possum and a drunk escapade with mice.

I rest when I wander amongst the dying ivy   gripped
the bunk as the submarine left. That   smell
me where I've splashed aftershave,   snaked
me once but never again. This is the   first
time lucky with no second chances.

Music for a Cold Snap

I have kept every coma on my   person
of interest to you, this headache, that   cough
up blood once more and I'm phoning for

the talking clock. This body is a   place
the tablets down and step away, let's   settle
down for a long hibernation. I am   better
not forget to leave the tap dripping, bones numb

from the cold snap of branches heaving a dry   laugh
track on American sitcoms. The clothes frozen on the   line
up for inspection, I still dream of my boots polished,

my bed made, my oppo face down on the   ground
coffee in the morning, vapourised dope at twilight,

a warrant officer shushing the room   choking
the throttle, counting miseries in memoirs.

Dripvangelion

⚡

Alex Mazey

I was doomscrolling one afternoon, maybe it was the morning – I'm not sure anymore when plugged into an information stream so appealing to my tastes and interests that time melts in a process that resembles the gradual mastication of a dark web gummy bear. Synchronicities steadily noticed in my life are appearing similar to the phenomenon of a winking universe and so it feels like I'm walking with God when experiencing a hyperfixation over Neon Genesis Evangelion (1995)[1] and almost immediately trippie redd & playboi carti - miss the rage (slowed + reverb)[2] appears 'up next' on my YouTube playlist which – if I wasn't paying careful enough attention – would seem so painfully insignificant as to be not worth mentioning here.

The synchronic connection that lies between Neon Genesis Evangelion and the slowed and reverb version of miss the rage can be found in an Instagram reel. This is perhaps my favourite reel of all time. To say, Dripvangelion[3] is a kino-reel for the serious intellectual, created by a reel-auteur whose name I cannot recall. It used to be people called me a drip as a child – and when it rained out on the street maybe I would get wet and people would say things like, "drips don't get wet, they only get wetter" – but in this world of linguistic reversibility it would seem like this word and its associated phrasing now possesses connotations of being cool, of having become cool – as in, so flavourful as to be dripping with sauce.

'Shinji your drip is so cringe!' A school friend announces in the subtitles, 'It's burning my eyes.' In this short clip of Evangelion, Shinji's classmates appear at the threshold of Misato's apartment door, where it is soon made clear that both Asuka and Shinji – and even Rei appearing with an emoji bucket hat as the memetic punchline – have broken free from the aesthetic uniformity of period anime through not only the time travelling capabilities of contemporary fashion but the sardonicism of Supreme t shirts rendered into the miscibility of the heavily-edited hyperspace in which we now live. There is an emergent miscibility located in a reel where Dripvangelion becomes the traction of Atlanta slang and an associated hip-hop sound juxtaposed with the radical authenticity we call cringe as made manifest through the disseminated catalytic of an edited anime classic in the brilliant alliance of those things once considered culturally peripheral. The cultural periphery should not be sustained in whole by the scrutiny of the cultural hegemony lest it become a mirror of that which it always challenged; and if Antonio Gramsci wished for the emergence of the organic intellectual[4] it may be the case that poor Gramsci was wrong only in the sense that those deeply aesthetical territories in which we now live would produce sardonic aestheticians who would celebrate shadows in the drip.

It could be said that anime and its associated cultural production are still situated at the edges of a heretical periphery, not least of all for falling outside of an anglospheric hegemony which remains both deeply cynical of practically everything it believes whilst at the same time advancing a separate notion of itself as operating at the absolute pinnacle of some ethical and cultural hierarchy in the smiley faced mutations of neocolonialism. The jouissance of this creepy ethicalism plays out everywhere today in the same way the anglosphere must lead the charge on the Green Revolution just as long as no one reports back on the cobalt mines that sustains it. As we descend further still into reality may God grant us the strength to enjoy the heresies of the cultural periphery whilst fun in analysis is still permitted. And so, I recall here those anime rich with slice of life and/or romantic genre conventions often based around surreptitiously ambiguous turn of the millennium time periods with narratives peppered with the beautifully illustrative mise-en-scène of the contemporary non-place[5] as once defined by

French anthropologist, Marc Augé.

It is perhaps demonstrable that the manifest of nothingness that also surrounds us in the present age can be seen as the quintessential superstructure of modernity just as Byung-Chul Han's chapter on thresholds, taken from his book on Hyperculture[6], leans towards this pervasive 'emptiness' as the staging ground for our 'hyperspace of signs, forms and images.' It is not inconsequential then that Dripvangelion also takes place within the threshold of Misato's apartment door, as previously mentioned, with all manner of reels and TikToks becoming the accelerated propulsion system of signs, forms and images.

There is a noteworthy scene in Neon Genesis Evangelion where Shinji visits a cinema alone. As the cold light of the film illuminates the screening hall we watch as Shinji's eyes fall upon a couple sat a few seats below him, his loneliness by comparison felt as an image almost palpable, the liminal space of the screening hall developing with a kind of pathetic fallacy. The cinema screen and its associated territories offer a sense of liminality par excellence in the way they so often stand as thresholds between reality and fiction. Shinji, seen in contrast to this couple – not to mention the scattershot of other bodies seated around him – is sat closest to an emergency exit, indicated as much by the faint glow of an exit sign above him. It is this green-glow of a stick figure running towards an open door which, as we know, haunts contemporary spaces with universal significance. And so, on one hand the exit sign indicates the designated escape route whilst at the same time providing the melancholic – dare I say, demonic reminder – that there is no escape from any of this. To exit a sense of precarious alienation is to perhaps enter another more terrifying than the last. Implicit in our semiotics then is perhaps the surreptitious reminder that nothing stands behind these systems of meaning other than that void from which we must always flee.

The deconstruction of this semiology is not to be confused with a call for its removal but rather provided here as an example of how our world might work in tandem with an entire system of surreptitious semiotics. It should be said that whilst the exit sign is a necessary part of any infrastructure it may be the tragedy of our time that in those signs that still recall our fragile mortality there may exist other subconscious universalities that pertain to a clandestine semiology of be scared and buy more popcorn. Consider just how easy it has become to think reflexively about metaphysical speculation as something quite silly (even cringe) since it is so often promoted – in the obsequious appeal to our greater intelligence – as an age in celebration of superficiality. Everywhere today there exists simulacra of the facile in order to conceal the real depths this construct has gone to in order to sustain something of its realism. In true Žižekian fashion it may be the case that the opposite is true and embedded in systems of complex semiology, reality is perhaps less superficial today than ever before. Further to this point, we may one day have to accept a superficial world which appears real until studied more closely over this world turned violent in its commitment to the aura of its realism. To say, the demiurge is turning violent – at the very least it has turned delirious as Baudrillard theorised – and if Vladimir Lenin once said, 'Every society is only three meals away from chaos,' then for our society chaos may result from three hours without WIFI.

It is like my mind also developed out of a necessity for noise and now I'm cursed with having to listen, through headphones, to stage three simulacra of a running bath just to get a wink of sleep. No longer transparent to reason and only emulating through the limits of my language what it was like to really live right now; operating as it were in synthesis with a delirious reality antithetical to peace. Like those ideas expressed in Emil Cioran's On the Heights of

Despair[7], it is my contention that every problem of philosophy develops out of this melancholic inability to come truly face to face with silence.

Second to this cringe inducing realisation, it could be argued that the ongoing cultural use of a word like 'melancholia' or 'melancholy' furthers the evidential bases for the compartmentalisation of meaning having occurred even at the level of our language. This is not to be confused with the popular use of a word like gourmet – for example – a term analogous with language games as they once related to the culinary arts today repurposed beyond many referential associations to the point where the term now stands as almost antonymic to its historical use. Alternatively, I have found that when people demand 'clarity' what they are really after is an 'immediacy' of understanding – and it is not inconsequential that Jean Baudrillard, writing in The Intelligence of Evil[8], traced the characteristics of the 'Virtual' to 'Immersion, immanence and immediacy'. In the hypercultural age of gourmet diners and gourmet candyfloss, the ongoing usages of this word – 'gourmet' – have developed as perhaps quintessential examples of Baudrillardian reversibility in language whilst also differing greatly from that phenomenon of what we might call cultural compartmentalisation; particularly as these occurrences of semiological repression relates to something like melancholia, which is to say, a word that once gave direction towards the friction that lies between mania and pensivity. It may be the case that what we have in these processes of compartmentalisation and repression is the gradual disappearance of what cannot be reterritorialized into seamless virtuality.

Certainly, in the hegemony of extremes there can be no talk of what lies in-between anymore since reality is today founded on the intermediate of multiplicities forgotten, and so even the liminal divide which was once so fervently discussed in aesthetics has been eroded to the point where a word like liminal – which once said so much about our place in the world – is intended to no longer mean anything at all, condemned as one of the many eye-roll inducing heresies of our time. It is like there can be no indeterminate feelings of the fringe and the unfamiliar in an operative reality without equivocation. The popular fixation on conspiracy theory is a likely outcome of this fully accomplished transparency since those conspiracies once considered entirely peripheral to everyday life had to become incorporated into the political economy in order to produce the intended result of integral subsumption. It may be the case that no extreme meaning will ever be achieved beyond the extremity of that absurdity now lived – and so all manner of unidentified flying objects descends from outer space. It is perhaps this sense of transparent integralism which also eclipses our ability to think with a degree of pensivity in a space where language also shrinks to meet the apparent demands of our lack. It may also be the case that a deepening of language is needed to best describe our world rather than the performance of its shallowing.

Before this repression in language, the seemingly mechanised partition of the sad from the manic – the almost ritualistic promotion of one without the other, as with a term like 'melancholy' – you could perhaps consider this word as a linguistic representation of reaction and remedy. To say, I am reacting to a melancholic culture with a sadness which is then remedied by its subsequent ecstasy, and so a feedback loop inevitably occurs in which consumers of the culture are steadily devoured by a process which offers a sense of perpetual escape. It could be argued that perpetual escape is the logic of reality today; no longer the misery of stasis as once theorised but the ecstasy of endless flight.[9] In this sense we are reterritorialized above the clouds in astral drift, circling a scorched earth, on holiday without a destination where either A) the repression of language has occurred or B) language is locked into

80

these generative processes of circularity. A third option seems more likely here, and it is one in which a pact is formed in the threshold between both A and B where the culture revels in the delirious miscibility of a little bit of both. The game here is always one of a balancing act between the two where the system now adheres to processes that can be considered rather self-regulatory. For example, the information age has banalised the art of decryption; the art of discovering what remains hidden in a world no longer all too human but a world made all too easy to perceive. Everywhere today it is a culture of disappearance made observable through a series of virtual reappearances; it is – therefore – deeply naive to trace contemporary examples of melancholia to graveyards and birds taking flight from frost bitten-steeples. That being the case, where does the melancholic experience (re)emerge in the world today?

It could be said that melancholia is contemporarily represented through an abundance of plushie toys cascading as water around a vocaloid in a neon drenched mode made in unison with the quasi-materialism of the arcade environment whose foundations seem built on the purest abstraction of emptiness and dissatisfaction; the shaky ground of electronic dance mats and the smell of stale popcorn crushed into threadbare carpets.

The Yameii Online[10] music video to PLS is perhaps the representational par excellence of a hypercultural gamble with the melancholic experience where 'please' finds abbreviation in Cyberia as both polite request and cry for mercy. Yameii's colourful miscibility as demonstrated in this music video and elsewhere has become a sure bet on the roulette of the culture. A wager on crop tops with long sleeves and hair made in the image of textures not found. In the lyrics to HATE IF UR MAD, Yameii's electronically synthesised lyrical delivery brings a self-described "prestigious aesthetic" representative of our perfect voidality; a means of

81

pushing the logic of the hyper-liminal – finding representation in the white space that surrounds her – to its natural conclusion in a world where the hues of hyperreality are that of missing texture colour. The server indicates that it cannot find the requested resource; therein, a two-tone in lieu of nothingness. This is without mentioning the miscible intertextuality incorporated into the animated accompaniments to Yameii's latest album – which includes both tracks discussed above. This intertextuality does not present here as casual inclusion for the shallow enjoyment of the listener but offers further evidence of an astrality that lives and breathes in another world as interconnected as this one. Take two additional tracks from the album, Candy, for example. In loading*: . . 。 (^_^) ft.deko we see race cars circling in opposition to one another upon a car park rendered with pastel-coloured cybernetics reminiscent of some Gibsonesque hyper-city made in allegiance with the hallucinogenic stylings of some Philip K. Dick demoniacal kawaii cyber angel type aesthetic. The amalgamate forming between pastel punk street fashion here interlaced with Yanki car culture recalls in my mind at least the meeting of two worlds as portrayed in Novala Takemoto's novel, Kamikaze Girls.[11] The sensation of speed and momentum given over to virtual worlds is later picked up again on venus saturn + offering the visual miscibility of Yameii meets Mario Kart.[12] Further miscibility in genre is demonstrated on back2me where electronic production and synthesized breathwork become seamlessly blended into midwestern emo in a weird combination not heard since Sewerslvt and Sadfem's exemplary remix of American Football's Never Meant.[13] To say, there is also a sense of weirdness operating beyond established frameworks as encapsulated by Mark Fisher in his text on The Weird and The Eerie.[14] Alternatively speaking, perhaps Yameii's two-tone space buns are merely Hatsune Miku's teal twin-tails as hyper dimensional accelerated pasticcio.[15] Perhaps there is so much cultural appropriation in hyperpop's transparent influence that some performative outrage against the genre may one day fund an entire PhD thesis.

Nevertheless, it would seem like my own experience with melancholia has been both exacerbated and paradoxically quelled with nightly karaoke sessions of the hyperpop variety where I have followed the algorithmic pipeline from Miki Matsubara Instagram reels to 80s Japanese City Pop[16], all the way to a new and exciting collaboration between izolma, mqrn and snorkatje[17] where nothing hits the blood brain barrier quicker than a cutesy voice shouting "baka" on the track whilst I'm farming cards on Genshin Impact's Genius Invokation TCG.[18] I take great delight in the ocular and aural self-harm; the real-feel sensation of my cat ear headphones producing a deeply spirited soundscape of the earworm variety only enhanced by retina damaging comfortable lighting and seizure warnings on the television screen. The view from my bedroom window – obscured by mist, as it is today – becoming that of a bridge popular with two types of people; Pokémon Go[19] players and suicide victims.

The aesthetics of Yameii Online and Pokémon Go are perhaps the natural continuation of video game worlds as they relate to the emergence of a mixed reality exacerbated in part by a few generations raised on interactive media. It could be said that a generation raised on a diet of video games is already predisposed to a disembodied experience of the world which still feels more engaging than anything we might still consider real. I recall Rick Roderick's eighth and final lecture[20] on the The Self Under Siege: Philosophy in the 20th Century (1993) in which Roderick casts his own mind to the image of a child angry at a Nintendo:

'I asked one of my children "Why are you yelling at a machine?" when he began to bang his Nintendo, and he looked at me as though I were a being from another world. And because of that there is a postmodern trajectory. I am from another world. I am still, as it were, caught in the modern. He's not. Why not be emotional with a machine? His peers are machine-like, we have already discussed that. I mean in fact what he sees on the Nintendo screen is his thrill of the day. That's the most active he's seen any simulated image that day.'

Thirty years on from Roderick's observations and the contemporary milieu is perhaps best captured in a strange collaboration between Mercedes-Benz and Mario Kart where partnerships such as these offer further insight into the fatal strategies of delirious miscibility taking hold of the cultural imaginary. There is in Mario Kart's hauntingly halucino-hypnotic world a sense of speed and momentum to mirror the apparent acceleration of our own. Having been thoroughly exorcised from an ideal sense of being-in-the-world, shadows hide in these child-like reflections which is precisely why the associated virtual territories still lend themselves to all manner of creepypasta and a cyberspace of cursed greentext.

Passing through a fever dream simulation of referentially de-sited farm life in Moo Moo Meadows or even the melancholically seductive intertextuality of Animal Crossing x Mario Kart 8, it is nevertheless always a sense of acceleration as conceived by Baudrillard in The Transparency of Evil[21] where the movement carried out on screen is always as circular as a race course; operating upon a Möbius strip of its own making. Demonstrably then, our reality is one of catalytic deliriousness pertaining to both material and metaphysical uncertainties having become thoroughly hegemonic in the way postmodernism cemented points of departure as endless destination. When considering what set of ideas made it out of the 20th Century, it may be the case that postmodernism[22] was always the enduring logic of this non-orientable Capital operating beyond the site of ideology; to say, from the bones of a dead God and a dying planet were forged a secular theology more perfect and omnipresent than any could have hoped. The pataphysical nature of what has become non-orientable may even develop the most rapturous of theological tendencies in the sense that the end of the world now occurs every eight to ten years.

In the end perhaps nothing is achieved and we are accelerating nowhere, every circuit taking place on a predetermined race course within a void which exists only where the Rainbow Road isn't. For further reference, the number eight on the box art for Mario Kart 8 Deluxe is a rotated infinity symbol in the form of a Möbius strip. I suspect many of us have played Mario Kart on a quiet Sunday and found it so repetitive and tedious at times that we wished we could stop the race for five minutes to conduct an urban exploration of Coconut Mall prior to its obsolescence; to enjoy a strawberry daiquiri on Peach Beach before the Great Pacific Garbage Patch washes up; to periodically enjoy these worlds for their aesthetic arrangements whilst no longer playing by the rules of the game. An alternative history of video games is perhaps one in which players have always detoured from given environments in an attempt to find some new and distant territory that is always visible but forever kept out of reach. A prescient example of this phenomenon is perhaps found in a player base who searched tirelessly upon the desolate landscapes of Shadow of the Colossus[23] whilst at the same time never really knowing what it was they were looking for.

Operating as a decadeslong series now, it may be the case that Nintendo have developed an all too perfect reflection of our world since Mario Kart is a game sustained in part by those things that pose as antithetical to the rules of the game; where yellow bananas, blue shells – and even short cuts – only lead us back to those predetermined and often delirious destinations which we may end up circling ad infinitum. What makes such aesthetics fun in contrast to detached circuitries of hyperreality can be found in the subconscious awareness that they can be turned off at any time; that we can be unplugged at the point of drudgery and still live. Compare this to our realities of totalisation without exit. And in the continued reterritorialization of this superstructure towards further totalisation in the virtual let us never disappear the sacrality of the off-switch and the exit – or even those radical acts of compassion which may find eternal genesis in the very peripheral act of feeding a bird outside.

Endnotes

1   Neon Genesis Evangelion, 1995, Netflix, Gainax, Tatsunoko, Japan, TV Tokyo, Hideaki Anno

2   slerb. (2021). trippie redd & playboi carti - miss the rage (slowed + reverb), YouTube. Last Updated: 07 May 2021. Available at: https://www.youtube.com/watch?v=thBrSMyzHwA Accessed 07 April 2023

3   SillySeeker Productions. (2022) Dripvangelion, YouTube. Last Updated: 06 February 2022. Available at: https://www.youtube.com/watch?v=eLBfTmNdBss Accessed 07 April 2023

4   Gramsci, Antonio. (1971). Selections from the Prison Notebooks of Antonio Gramsci, ed. and trans. Quintin Hoare and Geoffrey Nowell Smith. London: Lawrence and Wishart

5   Augé, Marc. (1995). Non-Places: Introduction to an Anthropology of Supermodernity, trans. J. Howe. London: Verso

6   Han, Byung-Chul. (2022). Hyperculture, trans. Daniel Steuer. Cambridge: Polity Press

7   Cioran, E. M. (1992). On the Heights of Despair, trans. Ilinca Zarifopol-Johnston. Chicago: The University of Chicago Press

8   Baudrillard, Jean. (2013). The Intelligence of Evil: Or the Lucidity Pact, trans. Chris Turner. London: Bloomsbury Academic

9   Mazey, Alex. (2021). Sad Boy Aesthetics. Wales: Broken Sleep Books

10   OSEAN WORLD. (2023). YAMEII - CANDY OUT NOW, including tracks and the associated music videos to HATE IF UR MAD, loading*∶．．。(^_^)　ft.deko, venus saturn +, PLS (-__-;) FT.DEKO, back2me *° :★ₓₒ , YouTube. Last Updated: 10 March 2023. Available at: https://www.youtube.com/watch?v=dH-AwGgmon0 Accessed 07 April 2023

11   Takemoto, Novala. (2002). Kamikaze Girls, trans. Akemi Wegmüller. San Francisco: VIZ Media

12   Mario Kart 8 (deluxe edition). 2017. Nintendo Switch. Nintendo: Kyoto, Japan

13   Sewerslvt. (2020). American Football - Never Meant (Sewerslvt & Sadfem Remix), YouTube. Last Updated: 07 July 2020. Available at: https://www.youtube.com/watch?v=Xm4lLN7pktc Accessed 07 April 2023

14   Fisher, Mark. (2016). The Weird and The Eerie. London: Repeater

15   Crypton Future Media. Who is Hatsune Miku? Crypton. Available at: https://ec.crypton.co.jp/pages/prod/virtualsinger/cv01_us Accessed 21 September 2022

16   rainbeary. (2020). 80s japanese city pop playlist, YouTube. Last Updated: 23 December 2020. Available at: https://www.youtube.com/watch?v=WCCovrKvAtU Accessed 07 April 2023

17   izolma. (2021). int tattoo feat. mqrn [prod. snorkatje], SoundCloud. Last Updated: 12 March 2021. Available at: https://soundcloud.com/izolma/inttattoo Accessed 07 April 2023

18   Genshin Impact (standard edition). 2020. Android, iOS, Microsoft Windows, PlayStation 4, PlayStation 5. miHoYo: Shanghai, China

19   Pokémon Go (standard edition). 2016. Android, iOS, iPadOS. Niantic: California, USA

20   Unism. (2020). Rick Roderick on Baudrillard - Fatal Strategies [full length] v a p o r w a v e   e d i t i o n , YouTube. Last Updated: 05 October 2020 Available at: https://www.youtube.com/watch?v=x73MNvENQr8 Accessed 07 April 2023

21   Baudrillard, Jean. (1993). The Transparency of Evil, trans. Benedict, J. London: Verso

22   Woodward, Ashley. (2009) Nihilism in Postmodernity: Lyotard, Baudrillard, Vattimo. US: The Davies Group

23   Shadow of the Colossus (standard edition). 2005. PlayStation 2. Team Ico: Tokyo, Japan

2 Poems

⚡

Stuart McPherson

Comfortable Room, Some Talking.

Loudness collects in places waiting to be opened. A slow breathing, like loam loosened around toes, buried feet. The anticipation of chrysanthemums opening in the sky that rise up like a cruel hand. The colours are beautiful. The way a palm squeaks the skin of a balloon as inside all the things waiting to escape are brought to the boil. I flinch. *I am flinching.* A naivety to voices froths from a bottle, froths over my legs. They are all so loud. Their noise is a dead body on a lawn. The heightening of greenness throttling the neck, the head, a sudden clapping of hands. Every year I light more fireworks just to stare at silhouettes. I tell myself that *delay is just fear of the unexpected* and so I hold them in my eyes, feel the angled grass beneath my soles. The thump of sound rising up and down again. From the ground across the cold sky or a cupboard door suddenly wrenched open to stark shouting. I remove my hands from my ears. Someone talks about rest. *Someone* is talking about rest.

Mediating Extinction Level Event

Children dance around a maypole. Red ribbon to yellow,
a navy blue, the sky shrouded with all our collective relief
flown at half-mast. *It must be the end.* A herd of liquorice
horses in the liquid field. This nostalgia smells like summer
salad. The way she used to roll the ham next to the egg, some
slices of bleeding apple. I wish I could have loved myself the
way I loved you. *Abrasion remembrance list* played in-staccato.
The blood runs away from the fingers, the pick-axe says hello
to the head. Fontanelles steeled in militaristic drum stroke
rudiment pattern as fireworks jabbed into cracks of pavement
are unable to dissolve. All hollowed out and spent. So quietly
seasonless. I hear the membraned voices downstairs creeping
in the yellow light of two conversant ghosts. Silhouette of
lonely bear twisted into tailfeather of comet, worn as scarf.
How many times should I disappoint this earth. Loose smiles
for every botched expression held in hand. How could I never
hold *yours* It is ending and the sea is perfectly still. We set fire
to our clothes. All dead swans knock together like wood.

1 Poem

⚡

Yousif M. Qasmiyeh

In the Aftermath of Writing

For Aaron Kent

I

i

... the opening for any inscription*

Where I am, the scattered trees are thirsty farmers,
myself hallucinating to reap words on a dry tongue

ii

I swear by the definite that is coming to its end, this is my life
slipping through my fingers.

A few more steps towards the end (never even) – the right
number my mother taught me in the dialect to beckon for the
Prophet's blessings whenever in need

I count
and count myself in the flesh then

A few steps towards the end,
towards the impending shadow, to come closer to he who, in
unuttered wishes, will one day lie with me

*... the opening for any inscription is Jacques Derrida's.

iii

Apart from the hissing quietness, no one to interpret the ethereal
clumps at my feet

iv

A gift is a thing to have
To give

v

I gift what is held in my hand
mud left on the edges and the odd fly

iv

The opening – the final palm –
for any inscription

II

So much they did to recount
what was yet to arrive:

From scribbles to crossed-out paths
my tentative breathing mistaken for meaning

Through the calcified lung or that which remains of it,
the shrapnel, well-lodged in hushed childhood

With scalpels and by hand, in labour, so long –
slicing the heart open to gut the baptismal eyes

Staring at the abyss before the mound,
the air raid poised on crutches,
above, not too high, as if it were a beast looking for a carcass

I sit across the chair before all faces, in-between is a slab,
an altar for the coming memories, not a feast.

III

That was before speech. When my mother, with a safety pin, would bridge the slit between one thing and its other. *An imminence is coming,* she shouts.

But now is the time I see it through the earlobe, like a trap for air and gaoled dreams. To translate silence in silence, warily she pinches the old blood to awaken its past, the buried and the underburied.

Rummaging the dry soil with bare hands, with the right, to nudge a path for the thing to break loose – not a cut but its afterlife.

How it pierces the flesh. Its home, it is.

IV

i

In a nutshell, no time to refute time,
I am mad, that is *majnūn* – a kin for
A foetus, a jinn, heavens caving in.

ii

Even those with a reservoir of tears cannot weep.

iii

With the mightiest grasp, I gather that which remains of sound, of
the vows I once made:
God! Grant me time, the last rites, the howling of a dying wolf.

V

Swallowing pills at once

Sometimes in order
The tailing until ends meet

Pondering the incoming train
Where people and things

Thoughts are spectres

My body in pain marshalled into a concrete slab
Patched over with pebbles and incompleteness

I look over, one amputated thought of many, a wandering beat

Tomorrow, when voices quieten, I will walk the same path alone

VI

Peace be upon the anxious being

The wished-for peace in tablets

in pills

In powder crushed on ancestral cloths
into more things

Congealed in the throat,
in panic attacks,
in deeply bruised limbs

Supplications for the unknown

2 Poems

⚡

Martha Sprackland

Ljubljana

Where I wetted a fingertip to pick up crumbs
from the zinc-topped table, before the sparrows
darted in to claim them, and wrote postcards
to the sound of church bells. Ljubljana!
It didn't matter that the war was still going on –
not at that moment. I had the pram safe
beside the table, a white manta draped across the hood
to keep the sun off. Time was such
that the bells finished their midday ringing
and began again for the one, and then for the next hour,
the gold hands rotating smoothly, in a mill.
But in other ways it was brief, my time there –
only as long as it took the waiter to sew me up,
for the sun to slip behind the spire.
The smoke of seven fires was visible over the marshes,
beyond the city's name the sound of celebration.
Then the bill came, and I was permitted to take
the pram – though the postcards I'd written
I had to leave behind, my Ljubljana being only a dream.

Look with your eyes

and not the way, like all children, you pick at the world – plucking buds absentmindedly and dropping them on the floor, never to flower; shredding paper (a document, a condolence card, a report, a thing of record, all the better), picking your sleeve to threads, your nose to blood, your nails, your scabs, your teeth, the wooden side of your bed, the skin off an apple; and you pull apart your food, pick pastry off a sausage roll, seeds off a sandwich crust, pith from a satsuma; must have everything separate, disparate, atomised and siloed – cheese on the side, courgette on the side, ketchup on the side, chips on the side, ingredients centrifuged back to their constituents, everything on the side of something else until the centre is unclear, life's main event diffuse, nothing whole or mixed but stranded and striated; pulling, stripping, reducing to dust and scraps, digging a way out of this world and through into the next... don't play!

Resistance

⚡

Jacqueline Yallop

The pelt of gunfire. No: rain; hail? No: gunfire. Hammering, like always. Then the blitz of shouting.

I'm sorry, the shouts were saying, far away, then close.

I'm sorry. I know it's early, but I couldn't wait, not even another hour.

There was quiet then, momentary, and in the night before dawn, time suspended, she slipped the bolts and chains.

Hurry, he said. (The gunfire fell about her like rain)

She placed her hand on the door to close it.

Only to sit with her while I fetch the doctor, he said. She's very sick. All these years and we've never asked a single thing of you.

His face of wrinkles was oiled by the early light or perhaps a slick of tears, or just the misery that befell him before he was born.

She collected her coat and hat and changed her boots, rattled in the passenger seat enough to shift her teeth, a button waggling at her neck like a premonition. Stones skidded on the track by the high woods; in the still-dark, the mountains pressed, old winters sinking from the peaks. He was chittering again like a startled bird: his mother had a pain in the chest. Tati had that pain too, around the heart often, lodged. When she tore at it, her nails broke, ripped from the quick.

Mounting the wooden stairs, she saw the mother kneeling, head bowed over the dangle of crucifix and the meatless knuckles clinging to unspoken prayers. Her skin was the colour of coffee stains. Already dead, one way or another. The sadness catching up with her.

She heard the van move away.

She was upright in her dream now: a wooden dresser the same as her own, a wardrobe wedged under the eaves, a heavy chest, the bed jutting onto the bare boards. Rabbits outside, crouched in thistles. The mother, the neighbour, just like (nothing like) the girl she'd been when they were girls together.

Tati took the neighbour's arm and raised her. A slow dance rehearsed long before when they'd found the neighbour's husband dumped on the church steps, a sack of trampled meat. The stench of him unpicked the years as they stumbled to the bed.

The neighbour surrendered to the crank of her breathing. Later, when the son came hurrying in with the doctor and the dusty light, Tati slipped down the stairs.

Walking home, high on the steep path, the toll of the hour repeated, rippling across the low fields and towards the mountains. Violets preened, the air sticky sweet, snaring old memories like flypaper. This was when she saw him. The way she'd imagined him, more or less. A decent coat and good shoes. A small blue car, blue or grey, door ajar, nested below on the flat land near the school gates, where they'd demolished the old houses and re-painted the Virgin.

He was, from there, from up there, falling into place: see it? The familiar angle of his shoulders, the turn of his head, his broad hands. Not like those other times. She'd been mistaken, then, most probably mistaken. (So many mistakes, rotting like flies on paper). She knows, now, she can't have seen him on those occasions. Except, perhaps, for that one night long ago, when she'd been sure she'd caught him edging the folds of blue moonlight, gathering sticks. He'd been undeniable that night, but had misted away before she'd pulled on her boots and coat. Even though she'd searched week after week, the barns and the fields and the ditches, not giving up when the snow fell heavily and the storms blew down the old walnut tree in the yard, he'd eluded her. When the winter passed, his footprints had vanished. The farm pieced back round her. From the state of the carcasses, she'd realised how the animals must have suffered.

From there, up there, she watched Armand stretch long arms

and return to the car. She heard the engine ignite. Good then: he was coming to the farm, the way it should be. This was the wrong place. They wouldn't know each other here, among the new buildings and the cleared land.

She cut across the fields in an ache of bones reaching the farm before he did and setting aside the morning chores to listen for sounds on the track. In the echoes from the mountains she heard something of him, but no way of knowing how recent such a murmur might be. No matter. He'd be with her soon, this time.

She placed a chair in the nook where the farmhouse wall met the wood-store. The Angelus rang and she closed her eyes. She might have dozed, her thoughts tumbling, the way pebbles fall when you loosen a large stone, the hours muddying in the slide, and under the dipping swallows in the noon yard, she slipped back to him, the way she often does. First, late spring, the sun beating over the ridge and the peaks carved into a timeless blue. Armand has stirred things at the farm like a squally wind: her father glares at this new boy across a length of pasture. There have been irregularities, eggs smashed and candles lost, the goat dried; not a bird to be heard in the nightingale copse. As she waits, he comes to her, leans across the table as she wipes the breadcrumbs, creasing the smoky air. Do you want to swim? he says, glancing at the back room where her father is resting.

It's twenty minutes' walk to the stream, another twenty along the bank in the seamless heat. They slip down to the bend of the river. He springs into deep water with a yell and sinks under the green wash. She goes behind a tree to change, emerges in her father's vest, her arms crossed tightly around her body. He never once glances in her direction.

The river runs from the high hollows on the mountain where the snow lies, cuts at them, icy. She feels the cold score her skin and sees, now, spray spangling against the hard, blue sky, and the glitter of mayflies, and beyond, the still black river. She remembers how they run out onto the bank and stand, face to face, his body dripping onto the ground, her father's vest an obscene nakedness.

When she looks again, the days are shorter already, veneered in grey. That year or another, no way of telling, but the soldiers already settled in the valley and her father missing the length of every night. The winter has come, hardly more than a moment, a silence; the field lies under the flat sky. Somewhere in the prickle of stubble, Armand takes her in her arms, his breath too warm. How many stars do they count? Such numbers are beyond them and they don't speak about what happens there, not then nor ever, as if there isn't time. She scrambles to dress. Armand laughs at the way she fumbles; he reaches to take her hands in his, rubbing warmth into them. Tati feels, now, his fingers entwined with hers. But still there's nothing to be said, too much set aside like summer fruit jarred for the larder.

The light slackened; Armand hadn't come. Tati tended the hens, then took the fattest of the rabbits from the cages, killed it, skinned it and cooked a pie, rolling the pastry to a waxy finish. This had been her father's favourite, spring rabbits gorged on lush greens, a sweet soft saddle, the fatty dew on the pastry; he watched her draw it from the oven, not as he'd been that summer when he'd led the men, wiry and strong, but as he might be now, too old, his face pinched. She placed the pie on the table under his bitter gaze then rested on the bench in the steamy smell of onions and spring grass. When she finally stirred, the dish had scorched a brown disc. She scrubbed at the wood with a wire brush but couldn't erase the stain. (A bad omen.) She rested her arms on the table, then her head in her arms; slept again.

She waited another day (or maybe longer) and then went in search of him. At first light, she took the van, working methodically from track to track, the old service roads to the mines, the loop into the mountains. He might be stranded anywhere; he would no longer know the paths. He might need her again, as he had before. The van laboured on the slopes, the ruts deep after the winter. She edged the bare land below the mountains, leaves already luminous on the sheltered branches; she walked where she could not drive.

Beneath the old beeches near the high well, a number of vehicles had pulled into the soft mulch, as many as eight or nine, one of them a minibus with rows of shaded windows. As she turned the next bend, she saw a group of people trailing the grassy path, such a cluster of bright raincoats and hats and walking sacks, that she braked with force and puttered to a halt in a slew of wet gravel. The van rolled back several paces. Tati pulled hard to secure the hand brake and got out.

She did not look at them, red and green and yellow, sprouting from the mountain like plastic flowers, because he was there, Armand, towards the back of the group, away from her. He looked much as he had in the village, except that he was wearing a lighter cap. She could not mistake him.

He would notice her, surely, and come towards her.

One of the men was speaking. He held up a map, ran his finger along the bloody gash marked in red. His words broke apart in the breeze. He pointed then at a signpost, the plaque alongside. Years ago they'd marked the old escape routes, a grudging tribute; this was probably why Armand had come here first, to remember.

Beyond, the land fell away to the valley; peaks rose, dented a blustery sky, but all she saw was the map and the line, the speaker angling the sheet against the wind, the clumsy red stroke bucking, alive, something in the throb of her brow making it uneasy, and Armand, looking at her still without expression, as though he did not know her.

After all these years, didn't he know her?

The man put the map into his pocket and went on briskly to the stile. He paused with his hand on the fence, swung himself over; one by one each of the group followed. On the other side they settled into twos and threes and marched around the sweep of rock as the path led sharply into the trees. No-one took notice of her; it was as if she was not there. Armand looked away to where the sky cut low through the gap of the mountains, the depression on the skyline like the slump of an old mule's back, still the border now, the crossing place (although she'd never been).

Tati returned to the van. The engine puttered; would not start. So she sat in the sloping shade, waiting. It did not matter. She had waited so many years, as though holding her breath: and this, she must have misunderstood this, how it was supposed to be, or he must have been too afraid to acknowledge her with so many people gathered, in case he was held to account for the past, in case they turned on him there and them. She had found him at the wrong moment. All those many minutes when she might have met him again, and it was not the right one, not a good time.

He would come to her privately, when he was ready. There was no need to hurry. And when he did come, he would tell her everything. She had set her mind to those final days in particular, many times, but had not been able to make sense of them. When he came back to her, they would remember together, and it would all be clear (and a relief).

So in the end, sitting in the van, she sees him again, as she must, in the glide of dappled shadows, a night worn through like a trodden patch on the rug. He's leading the family down the alley from their lodgings as she runs to catch up with him, always here, always in this same place. She should not be here in such an echo of clogs so far from the farm (is not permitted) but cannot bear not to be with him in the impossible daring that will make something of them both. She can help, perhaps. He registers his surprise only in the crease of his eyes. As she watches, the others squeeze by her, wrapped in scarves and shawls, the mother and the two girls, the troubled father who risks them all in this escape. She follows. Always she follows.

At the stone cross, Armand pushes on and she hastens her step to try to catch him. She slips past one of the sisters and then the mother; feels the unfamiliar rent of air as they climb out of the trees. She's forced to fall in line now by the nature of the path, and she can't see Armand, can't see anything except the blur of a coat ahead of her, a smudge in the utter dark.

The wind sweeps across the pleat between mountain and sky; the snow begins. It settles quickly; the rocks shape lilac-white as they approach. They reach the summer shelter and pause, the fog of their efforts rising. The woman sinks to the ground, her hands clutching the snow, and one of the girls bends over her. Tati stamps her feet until Armand hisses to make her quiet.

She stares past him into the vast open night. He strides away, and they follow, not the main route that brings the cattle up at the end of spring, but another way, clambering over boulders. They stumble and slide. A moon rises, a slender slice; clouds sweep across to blacken it. Either side, the peaks peel away, high and far, her father's farm, their fields and barns and hedges, all their labour, not really anything at all.

She follows the family up the steep incline, stones rattling underfoot, the crunch of ice, such sounds betraying them. She keeps her eyes on the indented footprints, the glistening bushes that scratch her legs, afraid to look up into the crackle of stars and the deep hollow silence of the old mountains. In all these years, there's never been a way of looking at what lies ahead.

When dawn came again, Tati was in the chapel. Squat, like a well-built pigsty, it sat in a square meadow, its low, flat belfry raised above the clutch of the trees. She heard the quiet clank of the bell in the wind (a sign perhaps). Kneeling on the bare floor, she felt the heaviness of a sudden waking; she could not muster a prayer. Her skin itched, burned; her face catching fire under Sainte Foy's unmoving gaze. She scratched. Her tears stung the broken skin. Under the gaze of the saint, the air twitched as if alive, or coming alive, like a cloud of midges swarming, a blessing.

On return to the farm, she cleared the chores, swept the steps, picked weeds while she waited. When the rain came, she settled by the fire, sliding, ashy, into a knot of dreams. Then came the attack of shouting, the son shouting, the door cracking, can you hear me? Can you hear me in there?

Every time they came for her the same way, with so much noise.

The mother was better, improving. They'd wanted to thank her, he said. Can you hear me?

She could hear him, the thud of his boots, his fists, then her breath like the rattle of dried peas. And a new sound, beyond or behind, years away: the putter of a vehicle on gravel.

Armand. (At last.)

The son shouldn't be here, had no right, not now, when Armand had come. She glanced at the burnt ring on the table, heard her father's whetstone whisper; outside, the men's voices, and now a tremble taking over like it had when she'd been up there, a farm girl, high up in the mountain with her heart racing, the assault raining from all sides so she'd had to run, plunging down through the snow to the trees, leaving him.

Tati snatched the shotgun from beside the sink and climbed the stairs to the attic. In the puther of dust, she crouched under the eaves. Above the front door, the slit of window puckered like a begged kiss, too narrow even for a girl to crawl through, expertly notched for the slide of a gun barrel. Below, the voices, below and around, twitching in her head, scratching like drowning kittens in

116

a sack. She leaned forward. The weight of the gun shuddered in her arms.

As the son stepped back, she would have him in her sights.

When she fell, they came for her, fussing and flapping. The other man, Armand, held back; in the shimmer of light and spinning dust, he floated, hovered. But when they decided she should be carried down, he clasped her in his arms again.

She remembered his smell, his warm musk. She remembered how strong he was.

They sat her in the chair by the fireplace. The front door hung from its hinges, the bottom panel splintered where they'd forced through, the yard beyond, her fields, the mountains breaking in.

The son crouched, asking questions. Armand was silent. She called out to him, his name, exactly the way she'd called to him that first morning to rouse him from his bed above the stables, but he didn't respond; instead the son placed a hand on her arm.

The fall, he said, had confused her.

What was he doing here (she'd shot him, hadn't she) peering and talking?

He stood up. The man, he said, this man, was in the area inspecting the septic tanks.

She couldn't shake her thoughts out; they clung, sticky, like old webs.

He was aware that she didn't like visitors, the son was saying, but this was necessary because of the lack of suitable drainage at the property.

But she'd been there on the mountain. She'd been with Armand. None of it had been his fault, not the way they'd said it was. The patrol had come on them without warning, springing from the dark like beasts, then her father's men immediately behind, such a fight that the mountains shuddered, and the family not able to run like she had, not knowing how.

The son talked about the drains.

Armand moved to the sink and turned his back. He had a hand on the tap. How long he'd waited to come home, what a stretch of years.

He didn't speak for himself, didn't explain, so she told the son: they'd blamed Armand for her poor father and for his, for all the men dying in the ambush. He hadn't dared return on account of such unfair blame.

'No.' The son's voice was small and tight, as though the room had filled with wasps: 'The betrayal was yours, the fault. You alerted the authorities as you ran through the village. When they found out, my father, all the men, went up to try to save you, the family too. They felt it was necessary. There was no unfair blame.'

His eyes fixed on her, clouded with an expression Tati didn't understand; a bright face even in the haze, like a drop of blood in the snow.

Armand fetched an old coat from the hook by the side of the smashed door and laid it across her shoulders, wrapping her gently in the damp-wool comfort of memories. When he was close, she saw how the years had disguised him.

She spoke his name again, softly, but he'd stepped away and was looking out of the broken doorway. He might not have heard her. Her voice sounded strangely weak.

She looked at the man – that man; Armand. He held his hands loosely to his sides. Something caught his attention beyond the yard, or on the ridge; he stood very close to the door, as though, already, he might leave. But there were so many things she needed to say, to ask, even now, when the words had grown faint, scratched in dust.

She called him again, as if he were across the top field, the dandelions banking yellow between them. She tried to rise from the chair but there were pains in her legs, her head too, the heat of the sun most likely and the strain of harvest.

The son slapped his palm on the table.

'Armand Roux is not here. This man is inspecting the drains.'

Armand held her gaze as the son talked. His eyes were familiar, his nose finer than she recalled.

'The patrols rounded Armand up at the mouth of the gorge, more than half dead already, God rest his soul; he wouldn't have made it even if they hadn't taken him. The priest came and told you this before the funerals. My mother came, too, to pray with you. We don't need to bother this man with such things – he only needs access to the drains.'

She held out her hand; he'd take it soon. There could be no doubt, not now, not after so many years. She was with him, there and then; she understood how everything would come right. The years flowed round them as they waited, snared in the still point of dusk.

Acknowledgements

Naji Bakhti's 'Zidane, Football and the War' was first published in *The New Statesman* (June 2020)

Naji Bakhti's 'I am Writing this by Candlelight' was first published in *The Guardian* (July 2020)

Naji Bakhti's 'Shattered Glass and Taxi Drivers' was first published in *Hadara* (March 2021)

Naji Bakhti's 'It is Not Sweet, Turning Back' was first published in *Hadara* (March 2023)

Stuart McPherson's *Mediating Extinction Level Event* and *Comfortable Room, Some Talking* were first published in *End Ceremonies* (*Broken Sleep Books*, 2023)

Contributors

ANDRE BAGOO is a Trinidadian poet, writer and essayist. His most recent books include the poetry collection Narcissus, the short story collection The Dreaming and the award-winning essay collection on art and literature The Undiscovered Country, hailed by Ilya Kaminsky as a work "as brilliant as it is startling".

A. NAJI BAKHTI is the author of *Between Beirut and the Moon* (Influx Press, 2020). He is currently a lecturer in Creative Writing at Aberystwyth University. His work has appeared in *the Guardian, New Statesman, the Kenyon Review* and *Discontent* among other publications.

MATTHEW FRANCIS has published six collections of poetry with Faber and Faber, most recently *Wing*. His work has been shortlisted for the Forward Prize, the Ted Hughes Award and the Wales Book of the Year Award, and in 2004 he was chosen as one of the Next Generation poets. He is Professor emeritus in Creative Writing at Aberystwyth University.

GAVIN GOODWIN lectures in English and Creative Writing at Aberystwyth University. He has published two pamphlets of poetry, *Estate Fragments* and *Blue Rain*. His most recent publication is *Creativity and Anxiety: Making, Meaning, Experience*.

STEVEN HASTINGS is a doctor in Aberystwyth, currently working in psychiatry. A former teacher and education journalist, his poetry has been published in a variety of journals, including *The North* and *New Welsh Review*.

KIT INGRAM is a prize-winning queer Canadian poet and fiction writer based in London. His work has been widely anthologised and appeared in magazines such as *Ambit, Magma, Acumen, Poetry Ireland Review,* and *The North. Aqueous Red*, his debut poetry collection, was published by Broken Sleep Books in October 2023. More at https://kitingram.com and @kitingramwrites

ALEX MAZEY won The Roy Fisher Prize in 2018 and was the recipient of a Creative Future Writers' Award the following year. He is a contributing researcher for the academic journal, *Baudrillard Now* and author of *Living in Disneyland* and *Sad Boy Aesthetics*. His poetry collection, *Ghost Lives: Cursed Edition* will be published with Bad Betty Press in Spring, 2024.

STUART MCPHERSON is a prize-winning poet from the UK. His poems have appeared in *Butcher's Dog Magazine, Bath Magg, Poetry Wales, Anthropocene, Blackbox Manifold, Prelude,* and *One Hand Clapping.* In October 2022, Stuart was the winner of the Ambit Annual Poetry Competition. His second collection *End Ceremonies* was published via Broken Sleep Books on August 31st 2023.

YOUSIF M. QASMIYEH is a poet and scholar whose work has appeared in *Modern Poetry in Translation, Critical Quarterly, Cambridge Literary Review, PN Review, Stand, New England Review,* and *Poetry London.* His collection, *Writing the Camp,* was a 2021 Poetry Book Society Recommendation and was shortlisted for the 2022 Royal Society of Literature Ondaatje Prize. His latest book is *Eating the Archive.*

MARTHA SPRACKLAND is an editor, writer and translator. Founder of independent publisher Offord Road Books, she is also Poetry Editor for CHEERIO Publishing. Martha's translations, reviews and fiction have appeared widely. Her debut *Citadel* (Pavilion Poetry, 2020) was shortlisted for the Forward Prize for Best First Collection, the John Pollard Foundation International Poetry Prize, and the Costa Poetry Award.

LAY OUT YOUR UNREST

Milton Keynes UK
Ingram Content Group UK Ltd.
UKHW022355080324
439162UK00004B/206